JANET JACKSON

A Real-Life Reader Biography

Kimberly Garcia

Mitchell Lane Publishers, Inc.
P.O. Box 619
Bear, Delaware 19701

First Printing

Real-Life Reader Biographies

Paula Abdul	Christina Aguilera	Marc Anthony	Lance Armstrong
Drew Barrymore	Jan & Stan Berenstain	Tony Blair	Brandy
Garth Brooks	Kobe Bryant	Sandra Bullock	Mariah Carey
Aaron Carter	Cesar Chavez	Roberto Clemente	Christopher Paul Curtis
Roald Dahl	Oscar De La Hoya	Trent Dimas	Celine Dion
Sheila E.	Gloria Estefan	Mary Joe Fernandez	Michael J. Fox
Andres Galarraga	Sarah Michelle Gellar	Jeff Gordon	Mia Hamm
Melissa Joan Hart	Salma Hayek	Jennifer Love Hewitt	Faith Hill
Hollywood Hogan	Katie Holmes	Enrique Iglesias	Allen Iverson
Janet Jackson	Derek Jeter	Steve Jobs	Michelle Kwan
Bruce Lee	Jennifer Lopez	Cheech Marin	Ricky Martin
Mark McGwire	Alyssa Milano	Mandy Moore	Chuck Norris
Tommy Nuñez	Rosie O'Donnell	Mary-Kate and Ashley Olsen	Rafael Palmeiro
Gary Paulsen	Colin Powell	Freddie Prinze, Jr.	Condoleezza Rice
Julia Roberts	Robert Rodriguez	J.K. Rowling	Keri Russell
Winona Ryder	Cristina Saralegui	Charles Schulz	Arnold Schwarzenegger
Selena	Maurice Sendak	Dr. Seuss	Shakira
Alicia Silverstone	Jessica Simpson	Sinbad	Jimmy Smits
Sammy Sosa	Britney Spears	Julia Stiles	Ben Stiller
Sheryl Swoopes	Shania Twain	Liv Tyler	Robin Williams
Vanessa Williams	Venus Williams	Tiger Woods	

Library of Congress Cataloging-in-Publication Data
Garcia, Kimberly, 1966-
        Janet Jackson / Kimberly Garcia.
              p. cm. -- (A real-life reader biography)
        Includes discography (p.), filmography (p.), and index.
        Summary: A biography of singer, dancer, and actress Janet Jackson, the youngest child in the well-known Jackson family.
        ISBN 1-58415-113-7
        1. Jackson, Janet, 1966---Juvenile literature. 2. Singers--United States--Biography--Juvenile literature.
    [1.Jackson, Janet, 1966- 2. Singers. 3. Women--Biography. 4. African Americans--Biography.] I. Title II. Series.
ML3930.J15 G37 2001
782.42166'092--dc21
[B]
                                                                                                                    200103886

ABOUT THE AUTHOR: Kimberly Garcia is a bilingual journalist who found her first job at a newspaper on the U.S.-Mexico border because she spoke Spanish. Her paternal great grandparents migrated from Spain in the early 1900s to New York where her great grandfather edited an Anarchist newspaper. Garcia has a bachelor's degree in English and Spanish literature from the University of Wisconsin in Madison. After graduation, she worked for six years as a daily newspaper journalist covering crime, local governmnets and Hispanic-related issues in Texas and Wisconsin. Garcia writes for *Hispanic*, *Vista*, and *Latina* magazines, among other publications. She currently lives in Austin, Texas.

Table of Contents

Chapter 1
Finding Her Star

Like many other seven-year-old girls, Janet Jackson loved to dress up and pretend that she was a famous movie star. So it wasn't surprising when she put on a backless pink satin gown and draped a long feather boa around her neck. Then she stepped forward, put a hand on her hip and said, "How ya doin' big boy?" in imitation of Mae West, a sassy actress from the early days of movies. The audience roared with laughter.

But unlike other girls her age, Janet's audience wasn't her parents and relatives. She was in the spotlight at the ritzy MGM Grand Hotel in Las Vegas, Nevada. Her audience was made up of

When she was little, Janet liked to dress up and pretend she was a famous movie star.

thousands of people who had never seen her before. The year was 1973.

The audience was there to see five of Janet's brothers. They had formed a singing group called the Jackson Five who became wildly popular in the late 1960s. They wowed audiences with their harmonic singing and synchronized dancing. Their first big hit, "I Want You Back," shot to number one on the popular music charts in 1969. It sold nearly two million copies in six weeks.

While the tremendous success of her older brothers helped Janet gain early exposure as a performer, it also had a disadvantage. For the first 20 years of her

Janet was born into a very famous family. Five of her brothers became wildly popular in the 1960s as The Jackson Five. All six of her brothers are shown here.

life, the accomplishments of her siblings often overshadowed her own achievements.

When it came to solo careers, Janet's sister, LaToya, enjoyed moderate success as a singer. Michael became the most acclaimed solo performer of the family. His popularity began as lead singer of the Jackson Five and grew even more when he launched a solo career in the 1980s. His album *Thriller*, released in 1982, became the biggest selling album in the history of recorded music. It won eight Grammy awards and sold more than 38 million copies. Michael's catchy pop songs and seamless dance moves, such as the moon walk, led critics to call him the "King of Pop."

By then, Janet had enjoyed success acting on television, singing and dancing, but she was still in her brother's shadow.

She distinguished herself in the early 1980s during a recording session with LaToya. Janet didn't like the song's arrangement. Even though she was normally very shy, she piped up with an alternative. LaToya liked Janet's idea so much that she taped Janet singing her suggestion. The tape impressed Janet's

For the first 20 years of Janet's life, her siblings' accomp— lishments over— shadowed her own achieve— ments.

father, who managed the careers of his children. He helped her launch a solo recording career.

"My father asked if I would like to start singing again," Janet recalled. "I never saw myself as a solo artist like my brothers and sisters. I asked my father, 'Do you think I'm ready? What if people don't like my voice?' 'Believe me,' he answered, 'you're ready.'"

Despite her father's belief in her singing ability, Janet's first two albums flopped. Critics thought the records weren't very good and claimed Michael's success was the only reason she was able to record them at all. Still, record producers—and Janet herself—believed she had hidden talent to tap.

"There's another lady inside Janet who's getting ready to come out," a record company executive named Jeryl Busby said of Janet when she turned 17. "I think she could be the biggest star in the family."

Sure enough, Busby was right. Janet underwent a makeover. She took voice and dance lessons, lost weight and worked with new producers on her third album. Her hard work paid off with her

> **Despite her father's belief in her singing ability, Janet's first two albums flopped.**

release of *Control* in 1986. Six singles from the album became number one hits on the rhythm and blues charts, beating a record that Michael set with *Thriller*.

Janet followed *Control* with five more albums, including four consecutive multi-platinum records. She also starred in two movies, *Poetic Justice* and the *Nutty Professor II: The Klumps*.

Janet also has given back to the community. She toured the country in the 1980s, talking to high school students about the importance of education. She's also donated some of the proceeds from her album sales to charities.

Today, Janet Jackson is one of the most successful entertainers in the world, possibly even more acclaimed than her brother Michael. She is no longer seen as the shy baby sister of one of the most successful families in American show business, but rather as an important star in her own right.

Janet has had a long and varied career recording albums, appearing in concerts, starring in TV shows and appearing in movies. Here she is in concert in 1990.

Chapter 2
Roughing it in Indiana

Janet was born into a large family that already included eight older siblings.

When Janet Dameta Jo Jackson was born May 16, 1966 in Gary, Indiana, eight older siblings already packed the family's crowded two-bedroom home: Maureen, 15; Sigmund "Jackie," 14; Tariano "Tito," 12; Jermaine, 11; LaToya, 9; Marlon, 8; Michael, 7; and Steven, 5. Their parents, Joseph and Katherine Jackson, had one bedroom. Her six brothers slept on three bunkbeds in the other bedroom. Janet and her two sisters slept on a pull-out sofa bed in the living room.

Gary was part of an industrial area near Chicago, Illinois. High unemployment, pollution and crime earned Gary the nickname "Sin City."

Huge steel manufacturing plants and smokestacks were a backdrop to neighborhoods of small, box-like houses, such as the one the Jacksons lived in.

Times were tough for the Jackson family. For several years, they couldn't afford a phone. All their clothing was either homemade or bought at thrift stores.

But Joseph and Katherine were determined to keep their family from the pitfalls of their surroundings. So they drew on their own strong family backgrounds in raising their children.

Joseph was born in Arkansas in 1929 and raised in Tennessee. His father was a devout Lutheran and a stern school teacher. By day, Joseph worked as a crane operator for a huge steel manufacturing company. By night, he played electric guitar in a rhythm and blues band called the Falcons. He passed his love of music and strict discipline along to his children to help them make something of their lives. Sometimes his children thought he was too heavy handed. He would push, prod and often scream to cultivate their talents. He was quick to criticize and rarely offered praise.

In the 1960s, the Jackson family lived in a small home in Gary, Indiana.

Katherine provided a counterbalance to Joseph's influence. She was a gentle and loving parent who often played cards and board games with her children. Born in 1930, she grew up in Alabama and also came from a religious and musical family. Her great-great-grandfather was a slave who sang in church.

As a young child, Katherine was stricken with polio and developed a limp. But she did not let her handicap deter her. As a mother, she walked to a part-time job with Sears Roebuck & Company to help her family make ends meet.

Janet credits both her parents for the strong work ethic that has helped make her successful today, especially her mother.

"I always think of my mother, whom I adore, and the attitude she expressed: 'Anything to make ends meet,'" Janet said. "When we lived in Gary, Indiana, when she already had given birth to nine children, she'd walk the winter streets to work at Sears, and this is a woman who, because of polio, walks with pain. This was when my father worked in the steel mills. Work is part of my genetic code. Work is in my blood. My response to adversity is always the same. Work harder."

Despite their dramatically different parenting styles, both Katherine and Joseph were strict with their children. The Jackson children didn't play much with neighborhood children. They were not allowed to use drugs or alcohol. They could not date until they were in twelfth grade and they could not live away from home until they were married. Their lifestyle protected them from the pitfalls of living in a rough neighborhood, but also isolated them from the world.

"I was sheltered, and there's both good and bad to that," Janet said. "The good was not getting into drugs and the alcohol…the bad was finally coming out into the real world and trying to deal with it, which was hard for me."

> **The Jackson children didn't play much with neighbor–hood children.**

Chapter 3
The Isolation of Fame

Tito, Jackie, and Jermaine showed particular interest in their father's guitar playing.

A broken guitar string changed the course of the Jackson family's life. All of the children shared their parents' love of music, and quickly learned how to sing and play musical instruments. Tito, Jackie and Jermaine showed particular interest in their father's guitar playing. Sometimes when Joseph was not home, they would take out his guitar and secretly practice what they had seen him perform.

But their secret was exposed when one of the boys broke a string. When Joseph discovered the damage, he stormed into their bedroom, held the guitar over Tito's head and demanded that Tito show him what he could do. The frightened boy took the guitar and dazzled his father with his ability. Joseph determined on that day to devote himself to making his sons musically successful.

Before long, the Jackson boys began performing in public, sometimes in as many as 14 shows each weekend. Meanwhile, their home filled up with trophies and musical instruments of all kinds. Then, soon after Janet was born, the Jackson Five—Michael, Marlon, Jermaine, Tito and Jackie—got their big break. A famous singer named Diana Ross got wind of their talent. She brought the group to the attention of Berry Gordy, the owner of Motown Records, one of the most important record companies at that time. Gordy offered the Jacksons an opportunity to make it big. But they would have to move to Los Angeles, California.

"I'm going to make you the biggest thing in the world," Gordy told the Jackson Five. "You're going to be written about in history books. Your first record will be number one, your second record will be number one, and so will your third record. Three number one records in a row."

Janet was just two years old when her father and five brothers moved out west.

Their father was determined to make the children musically successful.

The rest of the family followed 18 months later. In California, the Jackson Five's star continued to rise and eventually afforded the family a life of luxury. They also shared their riches with charitable groups, such as the United Negro College Fund and Food for Africa.

In 1971, the Jacksons bought a two-acre estate in Encino, a wealthy suburb in the San Fernando Valley. The Tudor-style mansion included a movie theater, recording studio, photography darkroom and trophy room filled with awards the Jackson Five won plus a gym, sauna and swimming pool. A tea room decorated with figurines of Snow White and the Seven Dwarfs and a zoo full of animals gave the home a fairy tale feeling while Janet was growing up.

While the Jackson Five's success gave Janet many privileges, it also isolated her from the world around her and even from her own family. Security guards and closed-circuit television cameras surrounded her home.

"There were girls we didn't know wanting to come over and visit my brothers," Janet said. "There were interviews, television cameras all the time, people screaming, concerts, photo sessions. I mean, it wasn't what you'd call a normal household. Let's face it. My brothers were teen idols, and sometimes we got sick of it. We had to have our phone number changed maybe once a week, and then these girls would still call. Who knows how they got the number? LaToya and I used to laugh because they made such fools of themselves over our brothers. And to us, well, they were just our noisy, smelly brothers."

Janet's brothers became so famous that in 1971 they inspired a cartoon television show for children. Janet saw more of her brothers on the show than in person at that time. She especially missed Michael, her favorite sibling and the one she was most similar to. Janet often tried to comfort her isolation with animals. Her family's zoo included a llama named Louis, two deer named Prince and Princess, an eight-foot baby giraffe named Jabbar, and a boa constrictor named Muscles that used to sleep on Janet's bed. One of her favorite pets as a young girl was Fluffy, a large mongrel poodle terrier she found at the park.

While the Jackson Five's success gave Janet many privileges, it also isolated her from the world around her.

"I guess I wanted to join them and become a cartoon character myself," Janet said of her brothers.

"I was amazed to see my brothers as these lovable cartoon characters," Janet said of the television series. "It made me love them and miss them even more. It also gave me the feeling that everything was all right. Cartoon characters don't have real problems. I guess I wanted to join them and become a cartoon character myself. I was a kid who found it easier telling my problems to animals than to real people."

Chapter 4
Dabbling in Show Business

Although Janet missed her brothers while they blazed a trail to stardom, she did not sit in the shadows waiting for their return. Janet dabbled in show business, starting with her memorable Mae West imitation at age seven.

Janet performed the same imitation and others in 1976 during a family television series called *The Jacksons*. The show's premiere marked the first time an African American family had starred in a television series. Janet's performance caught the attention of television producer Norman Lear, who offered her a part in a television comedy called *Good Times*. The show was about a black family living in a

Norman Lear offered Janet a part in the television comedy *Good Times*.

Chicago housing project. Janet played little Penny, who was the adopted daughter of one of the show's major characters.

Janet enjoyed her work on *Good Times*. The cast became like a second family, but the attention she received in her role as Penny further isolated her from her peers. Janet became so famous that she had to leave public school for a private one. Janet transferred in seventh grade to Valley Professional School. Many entertainers like Janet attended the school. Still, she had trouble relating to them.

"You turned sixteen and you'd get a Porsche for your birthday or some kid would drive up in a Mercedes," Janet said of her classmates. "It was like *Beverly Hills 90210*. In my family … if you wanted a car, you had to buy your own, but we couldn't buy one until we were eighteen."

Janet stayed with *Good Times* until it went off the air in 1979. She took another television acting job in 1981 on *Diff'rent Strokes*. This time, Janet played Charlene DuPrey, the shy girlfriend of Willis, played by Todd Bridges. Janet identified with the shy part of Charlene's character.

"In some ways, Janet and Charlene are the same," she explained, "but the

> **Janet became so popular that she had to leave public school and attend a private one.**

difference is that Charlene comes out and says whatever she has to, and I can't. Charlene shows her feelings, but if I'm upset and angry, I just can't come right out and tell the person. It takes me quite a while. That's the main difference. She speaks up and I don't."

By the early 1980s, Janet's experience in the recording studio with LaToya prompted her to see if she could make records as well as continue acting. But her musical talents took a while to ripen. Her first two albums were not well received. *Janet Jackson* was released in 1982 when Janet was 15 and *Dream Street* followed two years later. Marlon and Michael helped her write and produce her first album. Janet decided to work on the second album entirely on her own.

This photograph of Janet was taken when she was about 20 years old.

To increase Janet's exposure, her record company sent her around the country to talk to high school kids about

Janet shocked her family by eloping with James DeBarge when she was just 18 years old.

the importance of education. Janet herself had struggled with her career taking precedence over her studies. The tour helped strengthen her desire to complete high school. By 1984, Janet graduated from Valley Professional School. She quickly landed a role on *Fame*, a television series about students at a performing arts school much like the one she attended in real life. She played Cleo Hewitt, a young girl who wanted to become a dancer.

Soon afterward, Janet shocked her family by eloping at age 18 with James DeBarge, who was then 21. DeBarge came from another successful singing family. He and Janet had kept in touch since their meeting at a Detroit recording studio when Janet was 13. The two were married September 7, 1984 in a private church ceremony in DeBarge's hometown of Grand Rapids, Michigan. Neither of them told their families about their plans. Instead, Janet's family found out about her marriage from news reports.

"By the time I got home my dad was calling me from his office and everyone knew," Janet said.

The hasty marriage did not last long. The demands of their careers put a lot of strain on their relationship. Janet left James four months after their marriage, which was annulled a few months later.

"He would be in the studio all night until maybe 2:30 a.m. or 3 a.m. and I would have to get up at 4 a.m. to be on the *Fame* set," Janet said. "Sometimes, he would stay in my dressing room and take a nap while I was working. Sometimes, I would go to the studio with him. It was really hard and it just couldn't go on that way. You really have to have that free time together."

After she and James broke up, Janet buckled down and poured herself into her career. She took dance and voice lessons, and also attended a weight clinic to slim down.

Janet with James DeBarge

Janet returned home to live. She was stronger and more dedicated to her career than ever before. Janet's star was about to rise and she was ready.

Chapter 5
Success at Last

Janet teamed up with two of the hottest producers in the record industry.

Besides working hard on herself, Janet teamed up with two of the hottest producers in the record industry, James "Jimmy Jam" Harris III and Terry Lewis, to work on her third album. By the time they began working with Janet they had already produced many Top Ten hits.

Harris and Lewis wanted Janet to find her hidden talent by helping her break away from her past. They asked her to come to their Minneapolis studio by herself. When she arrived, they interviewed her about her life so they could write songs that brought out her personality.

"We knew we could do something with her," Harris said. "But she needed to get away from everything so she could let herself go. She was a bomb getting ready to explode. All she needed was the right fuse."

Harris and Lewis channeled Janet's energy and talent into an award-winning album. After *Control* was released in 1986, it became the top album on the pop charts, making Janet and Michael the first brother and sister to boast Number One albums. Besides the success of *Control*, its lyrics asserted Janet's control over her life. It changed her image from a sweet, shy younger sister to a smart, sexy and confident woman, much to the surprise of her fans and especially her mother.

"I'm just taking control of my life," Janet said. "That's what the album is about, control, and I've got lots of it. When I've made records in the past, I've usually been given a tape of a song, learned it, and then gone into the studio and sung to a completed instrumental track. This time around, I intended to be completely involved in the recording process, from the song writing to the playing to the production."

When her album *Control* went to the top of the charts, it made Janet and Michael the first brother and sister to boast number one albums.

Janet became wildly popular with the success of *Control*. And soon another man came into her life. She fell in love with Rene Elizondo, a Mexican native who moved to the San Fernando Valley as a child. Elizondo was a dancer, songwriter, filmmaker and photographer who collaborated with Janet on all her albums after *Control*. In fact, Janet took the bold step in 1987 of leaving her parents' home to share a place with Elizondo, and she dropped her father as her manager.

Janet arrived at the premiere of her new film, "Nutty Professor II" with her father, Joe, on July 24, 2000.

"I remember trying to tell my father I no longer wanted him to manage me," Janet said. "It would have been easier to have Mother tell him for me, but that was something I had to do for myself. I couldn't say the words, I was bawling like a baby, and finally he just said, 'You don't want me involved in your career.

Isn't that it?' 'Yes,' I finally found the nerve to say it, 'That's it.' "

Janet continued to thrive in her recording career despite some occasional bumps. She released five more chart-busting albums. She also appeared in two movies, John Singleton's *Poetic Justice* in 1993, and *Nutty Professor II: The Klumps* with Eddie Murphy in 2000.

Despite her demanding schedule, Janet found time in 1998 to visit with children in the SOS Children's Village outside Johannesburg during a tour of South Africa. Janet also donated a portion of the sales from "Together Again" to the American Foundation for AIDS (AmFar) in 1997.

But she had some challenges to overcome. One of them was a struggle with depression. The difficulties she went through were reflected in her seventh album, *The Velvet Rope*, which was released in 1997. It was not as successful as her previous ones, but it had a helpful effect on Janet.

"Singing these songs has meant digging up pain that I had buried a long time ago," she said of the album. "It's been hard and sometimes confusing, but I've

In 1998, Janet visited the children in the SOS village outside Johannes— burg during a tour of South Africa.

had to do it. I've been burying pain my whole life. It's like kicking dirt under a carpet. At some point, there's so much dirt you start to choke. Well, I've been choking. My therapy came in writing these songs. Then, I had to find the courage to sing them or else suffer the consequences of a permanent case of depression."

Another big hurdle for Janet was splitting in February 1999 with Elizondo, whom she had secretly married in the early 1990s. The two shared a beachfront home in Malibu, California along the Pacific Coast Highway.

Despite these mishaps, Janet kept her chin up. She had struggled with separation and mildly received performances before.

Janet with her husband Rene Elizondo, whom she had secretly married in 1991.

So it wasn't a surprise when *All For You*, the album she released in the spring of 2001, went straight to the top of the charts.

Now Janet has a staggering 50 million in album sales under her belt, and she shows no signs of slowing down.

"If Tina Turner can still perform at 50, then God knows, I just might try too," Janet said.

Janet and her band perform on stage in the Rhythm Nation 1814 tour in 1990.

Chronology

- 1966, born on May 16 in Gary, Indiana
- 1968, father and five eldest brothers move to Los Angeles, California to fulfill a recording contract with Motown Records. The rest of the family follows 18 months later.
- 1971, family buys a mansion in Encino, California, and a weekly cartoon series about the Jackson Five premieres on television.
- 1974, performs for the first time on stage at the MGM Grand Hotel in Las Vegas, Nevada. She is seven years old.
- 1977-79, plays Penny Gordon on the television program *Good Times*.
- 1981-82, plays Charlene DuPrey on the television comedy *Diff'rent Strokes*.
- 1982, releases her first album, *Janet Jackson*.
- 1984, releases her second album, *Dream Street*, graduates from high school, appears in the television series *Fame*, and elopes with singer James DeBarge.
- 1985, marriage to DeBarge is annulled.
- 1986, releases her third album, *Control*
- 1987, wins two American Music Awards for *Control*. She also fires her father as her manager and leaves her parents' home to live with Rene Elizondo.
- 1989, releases her fourth album, *Rhythm Nation 1814*; launches her first national concert tour.
- 1990, wins two American Music Awards and a star on the Hollywood Walk of Fame; secretly marries Elizondo.
- 1993, releases her fifth album, *janet*. She also sets out on her first worldwide concert tour and appears in John Singleton's film, *Poetic Justice*.
- 1996, releases *Design of a Decade 1986/1996*
- 1997, releases her seventh album, *The Velvet Rope*
- 1998, visits with children from the SOS Children's Village outside Johannesburg during a tour of South Africa.
- 1999, breaks up with Elizondo; films *The Nutty Professor II: The Klumps* with Eddie Murphy.
- 2001, releases *All for You*

Discography and Filmography

Albums

Janet Jackson (1982)
Dream Street (1984)
Control (1986)
Rhythm Nation 1814 (1989)
janet (1993)
Janet Jackson 1986/1996 Design Of A Decade (1995)
The Velvet Rope (1997)
All For You (2001)

Television

The Jacksons (1976-77)
Good Times (1977-79)
Diff'rent Strokes (1981-82)
The Love Boat (1984, guest appearance)
Fame (1984-85)
Everybody Dance Now (1991, special)
Racism: Points of View (1991, special)
Hollywood's Leading Ladies with David Sheehan (1993, special)

Movies

Poetic Justice (1993)
Nutty Professor II: The Klumps (2000)

Index